THE SONNETS OF WILLIAM SHAKESPEARE

The
Royal Shakespeare Theatre
Edition of

The SONNETS of
WILLIAM
SHAKESPEARE

Shepheard-Walwyn
London

This edition © Shepheard-Walwyn (Publishers) Ltd. 1974
Preface © Hersay Flower 1974
First published in this format 1975
2nd impression 1975
3rd impression 1976
4th impression 1980
5th impression 1983
6th impression 1986

ISBN 0 85683 013 5

Printed and bound in Great Britain by
Biddles Ltd, Guildford and King's Lynn for
SHEPHEARD-WALWYN (PUBLISHERS) LTD.
26 Charing Cross Road (Suite 34), London WC2H 0DH

PUBLISHERS' NOTE

IN this presentation of the Sonnets the text used is that of Thomas Thorpe's 1609 Quarto edition, the earliest extant source.

The only alterations made to the text as published by him have been in some of the letter forms: 'j' replaces 'i' where appropriate; likewise 'v' is substituted for 'u', and vice versa where modern usage demands it and it does not result in a change of the old spelling; and the long 's', which looks similar to the 'f' and tends to interrupt the natural flow when read by modern eyes, has been replaced by 's' throughout.

The calligraphy by Frederick Marns was specially commissioned for this edition.

Dedicated to the memory of Sir Fordham Flower,
Chairman of the Executive Council of the
Governors of the Royal Shakespeare Theatre
from 1944 to 1966.

PREFACE

SHAKESPEARE'S sequence of Sonnets was probably completed by 1599 but was not published until ten years later. Whereas the plays were written for public performance, the Sonnets were originally circulated privately among his friends. As the intense personal expression of his own deep experience they show the man behind the plays.

The Royal Shakespeare Theatre is proud to present this unique edition of the Sonnets. Through the generosity of the publishers the royalties due to a living author are being given to Shakespeare's Theatre. The book is dedicated to the memory of Fordham Flower, who loved this Theatre all his life, and those who worked in it, and who served and guided it with devotion.

It would be his wish that his work should be remembered in its historical context. His great-uncle, Charles Flower, founded and built the first theatre in the eighteen-seventies and guided the success of the early years. Under the chairmanship of Fordham's father, Sir Archibald Flower, the success of a brave local venture increased and the Theatre Festival became an event of national importance. Sir Archie met the challenge of the first Theatre's destruction by fire in 1926, and raised the money to build the present Theatre. Under Fordham's guidance it achieved international stature. His great gift was that he understood the needs of creative people and used his practical ability to provide the climate and conditions in which they could strive for their high artistic vision.

He, like his father and great-uncle before him, expended energy, time, care, fortune and devotion to this Theatre. The dedication of this edition of Shakespeare's Sonnets is made to honour Fordham's own dedication to Shakespeare's Theatre.

Stratford-upon-Avon   *Hersey Flower*

THE SONNETS

From fairest creatures we desire increase,
That thereby beauties *Rose* might never die,
But as the riper should by time decease,
His tender heire might beare his memory:
But thou contracted to thine owne bright eyes,
Feed'st thy lights flame with selfe substantiall fewell,
Making a famine where aboundance lies,
Thy selfe thy foe, to thy sweet selfe too cruell:
Thou that art now the worlds fresh ornament,
And only herauld to the gaudy spring,
Within thine owne bud buriest thy content,
And tender chorle makst wast in niggarding:
    Pitty the world, or else this glutton be,
    To eate the worlds due, by the grave and thee.

When fortie Winters shall beseige thy brow,
And digge deep trenches in thy beauties field,
Thy youthes proud livery so gaz'd on now,
Wil be a totter'd weed of smal worth held:
Then being askt, where all thy beautie lies,
Where all the treasure of thy lusty daies;
To say within thine owne deepe sunken eyes,
Were an all-eating shame, and thriftlesse praise.
How much more praise deserv'd thy beauties use,
If thou couldst answere this faire child of mine
Shall sum my count, and make my old excuse
Prooving his beautie by succession thine.
 This were to be new made when thou art ould,
 And see thy blood warme when thou feel'st it could,

Looke in thy glasse and tell the face thou vewest,
Now is the time that face should forme an other,
Whose fresh repaire if now thou not renewest,
Thou doo'st beguile the world, unblesse some mother.
For where is she so faire whose un-eard wombe
Disdaines the tillage of thy husbandry?
Or who is he so fond will be the tombe,
Of his selfe love to stop posterity?
Thou art thy mothers glasse and she in thee
Calls backe the lovely Aprill of her prime,
So thou through windowes of thine age shalt see,
Dispight of wrinkles this thy goulden time.
    But if thou live remembred not to be,
    Die single and thine Image dies with thee.

Unthrifty lovelinesse why dost thou spend,
Upon thy selfe thy beauties legacy?
Natures bequest gives nothing but doth lend,
And being franck she lends to those are free:
Then beautious nigard why doost thou abuse,
The bountious largesse given thee to give?
Profitles userer why doost thou use
So great a summe of summes yet can'st not live?
For having traffike with thy selfe alone,
Thou of thy selfe thy sweet selfe dost deceave,
Then how when nature calls thee to be gone,
What acceptable *Audit* can'st thou leave?
  Thy unus'd beauty must be tomb'd with thee,
  Which used lives th'executor to be.

Those howers that with gentle worke did frame,
The lovely gaze where every eye doth dwell
Will play the tirants to the very same,
And that unfaire which fairely doth excell:
For never resting time leads Summer on,
To hidious winter and confounds him there,
Sap checkt with frost and lustie leav's quite gon.
Beauty ore-snow'd and barenes every where,
Then were not summers distillation left
A liquid prisoner pent in walls of glasse,
Beauties effect with beauty were bereft,
Nor it nor noe remembrance what it was.
  But flowers distil'd though they with winter meete,
  Leese but their show, their substance still lives sweet.

Then let not winters wragged hand deface,
In thee thy summer ere thou be distil'd:
Make sweet some viall; treasure thou some place,
With beautits treasure ere it be selfe kil'd:
That use is not forbidden usery,
Which happies those that pay the willing lone;
That's for thy selfe to breed an other thee,
Or ten times happier be it ten for one,
Ten times thy selfe were happier then thou art,
If ten of thine ten times refigur'd thee,
Then what could death doe if thou should'st depart,
Leaving thee living in posterity?
    Be not selfe-wild for thou art much too faire,
    To be deaths conquest and make wormes thine heire.

Loe in the Orient when the gracious light,
Lifts up his burning head, each under eye
Doth homage to his new appearing sight,
Serving with lookes his sacred majesty,
And having climb'd the steepe up heavenly hill,
Resembling strong youth in his middle age,
Yet mortall lookes adore his beauty still,
Attending on his goulden pilgrimage:
But when from high-most pich with wery car,
Like feeble age he reeleth from the day,
The eyes (fore dutious) now converted are
From his low tract and looke an other way:
    So thou, thy selfe out-going in thy noon:
    Unlok'd on diest unlesse thou get a sonne.

Musick to heare, why hear'st thou musick sadly,
Sweets with sweets warre not, joy delights in joy:
Why lov'st thou that which thou receavst not gladly,
Or else receav'st with pleasure thine annoy?
If the true concord of well tuned sounds,
By unions married do offend thine eare,
They do but sweetly chide thee, who confounds
In singlenesse the parts that thou should'st beare:
Marke how one string sweet husband to an other,
Strikes each in each by mutuall ordering;
Resembling sier, and child, and happy mother,
Who all in one, one pleasing note do sing:
　Whose speechlesse song being many, seeming one,
　Sings this to thee thou single wilt prove none.

Is it for feare to wet a widdowes eye,
That thou consum'st thy selfe in single life?
Ah; if thou issulesse shalt hap to die,
The world will waile thee like a makelesse wife,
The world wilbe thy widdow and still weepe,
That thou no forme of thee hast left behind,
When every privat widdow well may keepe,
By childrens eyes, her husbands shape in minde:
Looke what an unthrift in the world doth spend
Shifts but his place, for still the world injoyes it
But beauties waste hath in the world an end,
And kept unusde the user so destroyes it:
  No love toward others in that bosome sits
  That on himselfe such murdrous shame commits.

For shame deny that thou bear'st love to any
Who for thy selfe art so unprovident
Graunt if thou wilt, thou art belov'd of many,
But that thou none lov'st is most evident:
For thou art so possest with murdrous hate,
That gainst thy selfe thou stickst not to conspire,
Seeking that beautious roofe to ruinate
Which to repaire should be thy chiefe desire:
O change thy thought, that I may change my minde,
Shall hate be fairer log'd then gentle love?
Be as thy presence is gracious and kind,
Or to thy selfe at least kind harted prove,
   Make thee an other selfe for love of me,
   That beauty still may live in thine or thee.

As fast as thou shalt wane so fast thou grow'st,
In one of thine, from that which thou departest,
And that fresh bloud which yongly thou bestow'st,
Thou maist call thine, when thou from youth convertest,
Herein lives wisdome, beauty, and increase,
Without this follie, age, and could decay,
If all were minded so, the times should cease,
And threescoore yeare would make the world away:
Let those whom nature hath not made for store,
Harsh, featurelesse, and rude, barrenly perrish,
Looke whom she best indow'd, she gave the more;
Which bountious guift thou shouldst in bounty cherrish,
    She carv'd thee for her seale, and ment therby,
    Thou shouldst print more, not let that coppy die.

12

When I doe count the clock that tels the time,
And see the brave day sunck in hidious night,
When I behold the violet past prime,
And sable curls or silver'd ore with white:
When lofty trees I see barren of leaves,
Which erst from heat did canopie the herd
And Sommers greene all girded up in sheaves
Borne on the beare with white and bristly beard:
Then of thy beauty do I question make
That thou among the wastes of time must goe,
Since sweets and beauties do them-selves forsake,
And die as fast as they see others grow,
  And nothing gainst Times sieth can make defence
  Save breed to brave him, when he takes thee hence.

O that you were your selfe, but love you are
No longer yours, then you your selfe here live,
Against this cumming end you should prepare,
And your sweet semblance to some other give.
So should that beauty which you hold in lease
Find no determination, then you were
You selfe again after your selfes decease,
When your sweet issue your sweet forme should beare.
Who lets so faire a house fall to decay,
Which husbandry in honour might uphold,
Against the stormy gusts of winters day
And barren rage of deaths eternall cold?
   O none but unthrifts, deare my love you know,
   You had a Father, let your Son say so.

Not from the stars do I my judgement plucke,
And yet me thinkes I have Astronomy,
But not to tell of good, or evil lucke,
Of plagues, of dearths, or seasons quallity,
Nor can I fortune to breefe mynuits tell;
Pointing to each his thunder, raine and winde,
Or say with Princes if it shal go wel
By oft predict that I in heaven finde.
But from thine eies my knowledge I derive,
And constant stars in them I read such art
As truth and beautie shal together thrive
If from thy selfe, to store thou wouldst convert:
    Or else of thee this I prognosticate,
    Thy end is Truthes and Beauties doome and date.

When I consider every thing that growes
Holds in perfection but a little moment.
That this huge stage presenteth nought but showes
Whereon the Stars in secret influence comment.
When I perceive that men as plants increase,
Cheared and checkt even by the selfe-same skie:
Vaunt in their youthfull sap, at height decrease,
And were their brave state out of memory.
Then the conceit of this inconstant stay,
Sets you most rich in youth before my sight,
Where wastfull time debateth with decay
To change your day of youth to sullied night,
      And all in war with Time for love of you
      As he takes from you, I ingraft you new.

16

But wherefore do not you a mightier waie
Make warre uppon this bloudie tirant time?
And fortifie your selfe in your decay
With meanes more blessed then my barren rime?
Now stand you on the top of happie houres,
And many maiden gardens yet unset,
With vertuous wish would beare your living flowers,
Much liker then your painted counterfeit:
So should the lines of life that life repaire
Which this (Times pensel or my pupill pen)
Neither in inward worth nor outward faire
Can make you live your selfe in eies of men,
  To give away your selfe, keeps your selfe still,
  And you must live drawne by your owne sweet skill,

Who will beleeve my verse in time to come
If it were fild with your most high deserts?
Though yet heaven knowes it is but as a tombe
Which hides your life, and shewes not halfe your parts:
If I could write the beauty of your eyes,
And in fresh numbers number all your graces,
The age to come would say this Poet lies,
Such heavenly touches nere toucht earthly faces.
So should my papers (yellowed with their age)
Be scorn'd, like old men of lesse truth then tongue,
And your true rights be termd a Poets rage,
And stretched miter of an Antique song.
    But were some childe of yours alive that time,
    You should live twise in it, and in my rime.

18

Shall I compare thee to a Summers day?
Thou art more lovely and more temperate:
Rough windes do shake the darling buds of Maie,
And Sommers lease hath all too short a date:
Sometime too hot the eye of heaven shines,
And often is his gold complexion dimm'd,
And every faire from faire some-time declines,
By chance, or natures changing course untrim'd:
But thy eternall Sommer shall not fade,
Nor loose possession of that faire thou ow'st,
Nor shall death brag thou wandr'st in his shade,
When in eternall lines to time thou grow'st,
    So long as men can breath or eyes can see,
    So long lives this, and this gives life to thee,

19

Devouring time blunt thou the Lyons pawes,
And make the earth devoure her owne sweet brood,
Plucke the keene teeth from the fierce Tygers yawes,
And burne the long liv'd Phænix in her blood,
Make glad and sorry seasons as thou fleet'st,
And do what ere thou wilt swift-footed time
To the wide world and all her fading sweets:
But I forbid thee one most hainous crime,
O carve not with thy howers my loves faire brow,
Nor draw noe lines there with thine antique pen,
Him in thy course untainted doe allow,
For beauties patterne to succeding men.
    Yet doe thy worst ould Time dispight thy wrong,
    My love shall in my verse ever live young.

A womans face with natures owne hand painted,
Haste thou the Master Mistris of my passion,
A womans gentle hart but not acquainted
With shifting change as is false womens fashion,
An eye more bright then theirs, lesse false in rowling:
Gilding the object where-upon it gazeth,
A man in hew all *Hews* in his controwling,
Which steales mens eyes and womens soules amaseth.
And for a woman wert thou first created,
Till nature as she wrought thee fell a dotinge,
And by addition me of thee defeated,
By adding one thing to my purpose nothing.
   But since she prickt thee out for womens pleasure,
   Mine be thy love and thy loves use their treasure.

So is it not with me as with that Muse,
Stird by a painted beauty to his verse,
Who heaven it selfe for ornament doth use,
And every faire with his faire doth reherse,
Making a coopelment of proud compare
With Sunne and Moone, with earth and seas rich gems:
With Aprills first borne flowers and all things rare,
That heavens ayre in this huge rondure hems,
O let me true in love but truly write,
And then beleeve me, my love is as faire,
As any mothers childe, though not so bright
As those gould candells fixt in heavens ayer:
    Let them say more that like of heare-say well,
    I will not prayse that purpose not to sell.

My glasse shall not perswade me I am ould,
So long as youth and thou are of one date,
But when in thee times forrwes I behould,
Then look I death my daies should expiate.
For all that beauty that doth cover thee,
Is but the seemely rayment of my heart,
Which in thy brest doth live, as thine in me,
How can I then be elder then thou art?
O therefore love be of thy selfe so wary,
As I not for my selfe, but for thee will,
Bearing thy heart which I will keepe so chary
As tender nurse her babe from faring ill,
   Presume not on thy heart when mine is slaine,
   Thou gav'st me thine not to give backe againe.

As an unperfect actor on the stage,
Who with his feare is put besides his part,
Or some fierce thing repleat with too much rage,
Whose strengths abondance weakens his owne heart;
So I for feare of trust, forget to say,
The perfect ceremony of loves right,
And in mine owne loves strength seeme to decay,
Ore-charg'd with burthen of mine owne loves might:
O let my books be then the eloquence,
And domb presagers of my speaking brest,
Who pleade for love, and look for recompence,
More then that tonge that more hath more exprest.
　　O learne to read what silent love hath writ,
　　To heare wit eies belongs to loves fine wiht.

Mine eye hath play'd the painter and hath steeld,
Thy beauties forme in table of my heart,
My body is the frame wherein ti's held,
And perspective it is best Painters art.
For through the Painter must you see his skill,
To finde where your true Image pictur'd lies,
Which in my bosomes shop is hanging stil,
That hath his windowes glazed with thine eyes:
Now see what good-turnes eyes for eies have done,
Mine eyes have drawne thy shape, and thine for me
Are windowes to my brest, where-through the Sun
Delights to peepe, to gaze therein on thee
    Yet eyes this cunning want to grace their art
    They draw but what they see, know not the hart.

Let those who are in favor with their stars,
Of publike honour and proud titles bost,
Whilst I whome fortune of such tryumph bars
Unlookt for joy in that I honour most;
Great Princes favorites their faire leaves spread,
But as the Marygold at the suns eye,
And in them-selves their pride lies buried,
For at a frowne they in their glory die.
The painefull warrier famosed for worth,
After a thousand victories once foild,
Is from the booke of honour rased quite,
And all the rest forgot for which he toild:
  Then happy I that love and am beloved
  Where I may not remove, nor be removed.

Lord of my love, to whome in vassalage
Thy merrit hath my dutie strongly knit;
To thee I send this written ambassage
To witnesse duty, not to shew my wit.
Duty so great, which wit so poore as mine
May make seeme bare, in wanting words to shew it;
But that I hope some good conceipt of thine
In thy soules thought (all naked) will bestow it:
Til whatsoever star that guides my moving,
Points on me gratiously with faire aspect,
And puts apparrell on my tottered loving,
To show me worthy of their sweet respect,
  Then may I dare to boast how I doe love thee,
  Til then, not show my head where thou maist prove me

Weary with toyle, I hast me to my bed,
The deare repose for lims with travaill tired,
But then begins a journy in my head
To worke my mind, when boddies work's expired.
For then my thoughts (from far where I abide)
Intend a zelous pilgrimage to thee,
And keepe my drooping eye-lids open wide,
Looking on darknes which the blind doe see.
Save that my soules imaginary sight
Presents their shaddoe to my sightles view,
Which like a jewell (hunge in gastly night)
Makes blacke night beautious, and her old face new.
    Loe thus by day my lims, by night my mind,
    For thee, and for my selfe, noe quiet finde.

28

How can I then returne in happy plight
That am debard the benifit of rest?
When daies oppression is not eazd by night,
But day by night and night by day oprest.
And each (though enimes to ethers raigne)
Doe in consent shake hands to torture me,
The one by toyle, the other to complaine
How far I toyle, still farther off from thee.
I tell the Day to please him thou art bright,
And do'st him grace when clouds doe blot the heaven:
So flatter I the swart complexiond night,
When sparkling stars twire not thou guil'st th'eaven.
  But day doth daily draw my sorrowes longer, (stronger
  And night doth nightly make greefes length seeme

When in disgrace with Fortune and mens eyes,
I all alone beweepe my out-cast state,
And trouble deafe heaven with my bootlesse cries,
And looke upon my selfe and curse my fate.
Wishing me like to one more rich in hope,
Featur'd like him, like him with friends possest,
Desiring this mans art, and that mans skope,
With what I most injoy contented least,
Yet in these thoughts my selfe almost despising,
Haplye I thinke on thee, and then my state,
(Like to the Larke at breake of daye arising)
From sullen earth sings himns at Heavens gate,
  For thy sweet love remembred such welth brings,
  That then I skorne to change my state with Kings.

When to the Sessions of sweet silent thought,
I sommon up remembrance of things past,
I sigh the lacke of many a thing I sought,
And with old woes new waile my deare times waste:
Then can I drowne an eye (un-us'd to flow)
For precious friends hid in deaths dateles night,
And weepe a fresh loves long since canceld woe,
And mone th'expence of many a vannisht sight.
Then can I greeve at greevances fore-gon,
And heavily from woe to woe tell ore
The sad account of fore-bemoned mone,
Which I new pay, as if not payd before.
    But if the while I thinke on thee (deare friend)
    All losses are restord, and sorrowes end.

31

Thy bosome is indeared with all hearts,
Which I by lacking have supposed dead,
And there raignes Love and all Loves loving parts,
And all those friends which I thought buried.
How many a holy and obsequious teare
Hath deare religious love stolne from mine eye,
As interest of the dead, which now appeare,
But things remov'd that hidden in there lie.
Thou art the grave where buried love doth live,
Hung with the tropheis of my lovers gon,
Who all their parts of me to thee did give,
That due of many, now is thine alone.
    Their images I lov'd, I view in thee,
    And thou (all they) hast all the all of me.

If thou survive my well contented daie,
When that churle death my bones with dust shall cover
And shalt by fortune once more re-survay:
These poore rude lines of thy deceased Lover:
Compare them with the bett'ring of the time,
And though they be out-stript by every pen,
Reserve them for my love, not for their rime,
Exceeded by the hight of happier men.
Oh then voutsafe me but this loving thought,
Had my friends Muse growne with this growing age,
A dearer birth then this his love had brought
To march in ranckes of better equipage:
    But since he died and Poets better prove,
    Theirs for their stile ile read, his for his love.

Full many a glorious morning have I seene,
Flatter the mountaine tops with soveraine eie,
Kissing with golden face the meddowes greene;
Guilding pale streames with heavenly alcumy:
Anon permit the basest cloudes to ride,
With ougly rack on his celestiall face,
And from the for-lorne world his visage hide
Stealing unseene to west with this disgrace:
Even so my Sunne one early morne did shine,
With all triumphant splendor on my brow,
But out alack, he was but one houre mine,
The region cloude hath mask'd him from me now.
 Yet him for this, my love no whit disdaineth,
 Suns of the world may staine, whẽ heavens sun stainteh.

Why didst thou promise such a beautious day,
And make me travaile forth without my cloake,
To let bace cloudes ore-take me in my way,
Hiding thy brav'ry in their rotten smoke.
'Tis not enough that through the cloude thou breake,
To dry the raine on my storme-beaten face,
For no man well of such a salve can speake,
That heales the wound, and cures not the disgrace:
Nor can thy shame give phisicke to my griefe,
Though thou repent, yet I have still the losse,
Th'offenders sorrow lends but weake reliefe
To him that beares the strong offenses losse.
    Ah but those teares are pearle which thy love sheeds,
    And they are ritch, and ransome all ill deeds.

No more bee greev'd at that which thou hast done,
Roses have thornes, and silver fountaines mud,
Cloudes and eclipses staine both Moone and Sunne,
And loathsome canker lives in sweetest bud.
All men make faults, and even I in this,
Authorizing thy trespas with compare,
My selfe corrupting salving thy amisse,
Excusing their sins more then their sins are:
For to thy sensuall fault I bring in sence,
Thy adverse party is thy Advocate,
And gainst my selfe a lawfull plea commence,
Such civill war is in my love and hate,
    That I an accessary needs must be,
    To that sweet theefe which sourely robs from me,

Let me confesse that we two must be twaine,
Although our undevided loves are one:
So shall those blots that do with me remaine,
Without thy helpe, by me be borne alone.
In our two loves there is but one respect,
Though in our lives a seperable spight,
Which though it alter not loves sole effect,
Yet doth it steale sweet houres from loves delight,
I may not ever-more acknowledge thee,
Least my bewailed guilt should do thee shame,
Nor thou with publike kindnesse honour me,
Unlesse thou take that honour from thy name:
    But doe not so, I love thee in such sort,
    As thou being mine, mine is thy good report.

As a decrepit father takes delight,
To see his active childe do deeds of youth,
So I, made lame by Fortunes dearest spight
Take all my comfort of thy worth and truth.
For whether beauty, birth, or wealth, or wit,
Or any of these all, or all, or more
Intitled in their parts, do crowned sit,
I make my love ingrafted to this store:
So then I am not lame, poore, nor dispis'd,
Whilst that this shadow doth such substance give,
That I in thy abundance am suffic'd,
And by a part of all thy glory live:
    Looke what is best, that best I wish in thee,
    This wish I have, then ten times happy me.

38

How can my Muse want subject to invent
While thou dost breath that poor'st into my verse,
Thine owne sweet argument, to excellent,
For every vulgar paper to rehearse:
Oh give thy selfe the thankes if ought in me,
Worthy perusal stand against thy sight,
For who's so dumbe that cannot write to thee,
When thou thy selfe dost give invention light?
Be thou the tenth Muse, ten times more in worth
Then those old nine which rimers invocate,
And he that calls on thee, let him bring forth
Eternal numbers to out-live long date.
  If my slight Muse doe please these curious daies,
  The paine be mine, but thine shal be the praise.

Oh how thy worth with manners may I singe,
When thou art all the better part of me?
What can mine owne praise to mine owne selfe bring;
And what is't but mine owne when I praise thee,
Even for this, let us devided live,
And our deare love loose name of single one,
That by this seperation I may give:
That due to thee which thou deserv'st alone:
Oh absence what a torment wouldst thou prove,
Were it not thy soure leisure gave sweet leave,
To entertaine the time with thoughts of love,
Which time and thoughts so sweetly dost deceive.
    And that thou teachest how to make one twaine,
    By praising him here who doth hence remaine.

Take all my loves, my love, yea take them all,
What hast thou then more then thou hadst before?
No love, my love, that thou maist true love call,
All mine was thine, before thou hadst this more:
Then if for my love, thou my love receivest,
I cannot blame thee, for my love thou usest,
But yet be blam'd, if thou this selfe deceavest
By wilfull taste of what thy selfe refusest.
I doe forgive thy robb'rie gentle theefe
Although thou steale thee all my poverty:
And yet love knowes it is a greater griefe
To beare loves wrong, then hates knowne injury.
    Lascivious grace, in whom all il wel showes,
    Kill me with spights yet we must not be foes.

41

Those pretty wrongs that liberty commits,
When I am some-time absent from thy heart,
Thy beautie, and thy yeares full well befits,
For still temptation followes where thou art.
Gentle thou art, and therefore to be wonne,
Beautious thou art, therefore to be assailed.
And when a woman woes, what womans sonne,
Will sourely leave her till he have prevailed.
Aye me, but yet thou mighst my seate forbeare,
And chide thy beauty, and thy straying youth,
Who lead thee in their ryot even there
Where thou art forst to breake a two-fold truth:
　　Hers by thy beauty tempting her to thee,
　　Thine by thy beautie beeing false to me.

That thou hast her it is not all my griefe,
And yet it may be said I lov'd her deerely,
That she hath thee is of my wayling cheefe,
A losse in love that touches me more neerely.
Loving offendors thus I will excuse yee,
Thou doost love her, because thou knowst I love her,
And for my sake even so doth she abuse me,
Suffring my friend for my sake to approove her,
If I loose thee, my losse is my loves gaine,
And loosing her, my friend hath found that losse,
Both finde each other, and I loose both twaine,
And both for my sake lay on me this crosse,
    But here's the joy, my friend and I are one,
    Sweete flattery, then she loves but me alone.

When most I winke then doe mine eyes best see,
For all the day they view things unrespected,
But when I sleepe, in dreames they looke on thee,
And darkely bright, are bright in darke directed.
Then thou whose shaddow shaddowes doth make bright,
How would thy shadowes forme, forme happy show,
To the cleere day with thy much cleerer light,
When to un-seeing eyes thy shade shines so?
How would (I say) mine eyes be blessed made,
By looking on thee in the living day?
When in dead night their faire imperfect shade,
Through heavy sleepe on sightlesse eyes doth stay?
  All dayes are nights to see till I see thee,
  And nights bright daies when dreams do shew thee me,

44

If the dull substance of my flesh were thought,
Injurious distance should not stop my way,
For then dispight of space I would be brought,
From limits farre remote, where thou doost stay,
No matter then although my foote did stand
Upon the farthest earth remoov'd from thee,
For nimble thought can jumpe both sea and land,
As soone as thinke the place where he would be.
But ah, thought kills me that I am not thought
To leape large lengths of miles when thou art gone,
But that so much of earth and water wrought,
I must attend, times leasure with my mone.
    Receiving naughts by elements so sloe,
    But heavie teares, badges of eithers woe.

The other two, slight ayre, and purging fire,
Are both with thee, where ever I abide,
The first my thought, the other my desire,
These present absent with swift motion slide.
For when these quicker Elements are gone
In tender Embassie of love to thee,
My life being made of foure, with two alone,
Sinkes downe to death, opprest with melancholie.
Untill lives composition be recured,
By those swift messengers return'd from thee,
Who even but now come back againe assured,
Of their faire health, recounting it to me.
    This told, I joy, but then no longer glad,
    I send them back againe and straight grow sad.

Mine eye and heart are at a mortall warre,
How to devide the conquest of thy sight,
Mine eye, my heart their pictures sight would barre,
My heart, mine eye the freeedome of that right,
My heart doth plead that thou in him doost lye,
(A closet never pearst with christall eyes)
But the defendant doth that plea deny,
And sayes in him their faire appearance lyes.
To side this title is impannelled
A quest of thoughts, all tennants to the heart,
And by their verdict is determined
The cleere eyes moyitie, and the deare hearts part.
  As thus, mine eyes due is their outward part,
  And my hearts right, their inward love of heart.

Betwixt mine eye and heart a league is tooke,
And each doth good turnes now unto the other,
When that mine eye is famisht for a looke,
Or heart in love with sighes himselfe doth smother;
With my loves picture then my eye doth feast,
And to the painted banquet bids my heart:
An other time mine eye is my hearts guest,
And in his thoughts of love doth share a part.
So either by thy picture or my love,
Thy seife away, are present still with me,
For thou nor farther then my thoughts canst move,
And I am still with them, and they with thee.
    Or if they sleepe, thy picture in my sight
    Awakes my heart, to hearts and eyes delight.

How carefull was I when I tooke my way,
Each trifle under truest barres to thrust,
That to my use it might un-used stay
From hands of falsehood, in sure wards of trust?
But thou, to whom my jewels trifles are,
Most worthy comfort, now my greatest griefe,
Thou best of deerest, and mine onely care,
Art left the prey of every vulgar theefe.
Thee have I not lockt up in any chest,
Save where thou art not, though I feele thou art,
Within the gentle closure of my brest,
From whence at pleasure thou maist come and part,
    And even thence thou wilt be stolne I feare,
    For truth prooves theevish for a prize so deare.

Against that time (if ever that time come)
When I shall see thee frowne on my defects,
When as thy love hath cast his utmost summe,
Cauld to that audite by advis'd respects,
Against that time when thou shalt strangely passe,
And scarcely greete me with that sunne thine eye,
When love converted from the thing it was
Shall reasons finde of setled gravitie.
Against that time do I insconce me here
Within the knowledge of mine owne desart,
And this my hand, against my selfe upreare,
To guard the lawfull reasons on thy part,
   To leave poore me, thou hast the strength of lawes,
   Since why to love, I can alledge no cause.

How heavie doe I journey on the way,
When what I seeke (my wearie travels end)
Doth teach that ease and that repose to say
Thus farre the miles are measurde from thy friend.
The beast that beares me, tired with my woe,
Plods duly on, to beare that waight in me,
As if by some instinct the wretch did know
His rider lov'd not speed being made from thee:
The bloody spurre cannot provoke him on,
That some-times anger thrusts into his hide,
Which heavily he answers with a grone,
More sharpe to me then spurring to his side,
  For that same grone doth put this in my mind,
  My greefe lies onward and my joy behind.

Thus can my love excuse the slow offence,
Of my dull bearer, when from thee I speed,
From where thou art, why shoulld I hast me thence,
Till I returne of posting is noe need.
O what excuse will my poore beast then find,
When swift extremity can seeme but slow,
Then should I spurre though mounted on the wind,
In winged speed no motion shall I know,
Then can no horse with my desire keepe pace,
Therefore desire (of perfects love being made)
Shall naigh noe dull flesh in his fiery race,
But love, for love, thus shall excuse my jade,
    Since from thee going, he went wilfull slow,
    Towards thee ile run, and give him leave to goe.

So am I as the rich whose blessed key,
Can bring him to his sweet up-locked treasure,
The which he will not ev'ry hower survay,
For blunting the fine point of seldome pleasure.
Therefore are feasts so sollemne and so rare,
Since sildom comming in the long yeare set,
Like stones of worth they thinly placed are,
Or captaine Jewells in the carconet.
So is the time that keepes you as my chest,
Or as the ward-robe which the robe doth hide,
To make some speciall instant speciall blest,
By new unfoulding his imprison'd pride.
  Blessed are you whose worthinesse gives skope,
  Being had to tryumph, being lackt to hope.

What is your substance, whereof are you made,
That millions of strange shaddowes on you tend?
Since every one, hath every one, one shade,
And you but one, can every shaddow lend:
Describe *Adonis* and the counterfet,
Is poorely immitated after you,
On *Hellens* cheeke all art of beautie set,
And you in *Grecian* tires are painted new:
Speake of the spring, and foyzon of the yeare,
The one doth shaddow of your beautie show,
The other as your bountie doth appeare,
And you in every blessed shape we know.
　　In all externall grace you have some part,
　　But you like none, none you for constant heart.

Oh how much more doth beautie beautious seeme,
By that sweet ornament which truth doth give,
The Rose lookes faire, but fairer we it deeme
For that sweet odor, which doth in it live:
The Canker bloomes have full as deepe a die,
As the perfumed tincture of the Roses,
Hang on such thornes, and play as wantonly,
When sommers breath their masked buds discloses:
But for their virtue only is their show,
They live unwoo'd, and unrespected fade,
Die to themselves. Sweet Roses doe not so,
Of their sweet deathes, are sweetest odors made:
  And so of you, beautious and lovely youth,
  When that shall vade, by verse distils your truth.

Not marble, nor the guilded monument,
Of Princes shall out-live this powrefull rime,
But you shall shine more bright in these contents
Then unswept stone, besmeer'd with sluttish time.
When wastefull warre shall *Statues* over-turne,
And broiles roote out the worke of masonry,
Nor *Mars* his sword, nor warres quick fire shall burne:
The living record of your memory.
Gainst death, and all oblivious emnity
Shall you pace forth, your praise shall stil finde roome,
Even in the eyes of all posterity
That weare this world out to the ending doome.
      So til the judgement that your selfe arise,
      You live in this, and dwell in lovers eies.

56

Sweet love renew thy force, be it not said
Thy edge should blunter be then apetite,
Which but too daie by feeding is alaied,
To morrow sharpned in his former might.
So love be thou, although too daie thou fill
Thy hungrie eies, even till they winck with fulnesse,
Too morrow see againe, and doe not kill
The spirit of Love, with a perpetual dulnesse:
Let this sad *Intrim* like the Ocean be
Which parts the shore, where two contracted new,
Come daily to the banckes, that when they see:
Returne of love, more blest may be the view.
    As cal it Winter, which being ful of care,
    Makes Sõmers welcome, thrice more wish'd, more rare.

Being your slave what should I doe but tend,
Upon the houres, and times of your desire?
I have no precious time at al to spend;
Nor services to doe til you require.
Nor dare I chide the world without end houre,
Whilst I (my soveraine) watch the clock for you,
Nor thinke the bitternesse of absence sowre,
When you have bid your servant once adieue.
Nor dare I question with my jealious thought,
Where you may be, or your affaires suppose,
But like a sad slave stay and thinke of nought
Save where you are, how happy you make those.
    So true a foole is love, that in your Will,
    (Though you doe any thing) he thinkes no ill.

58

That God forbid, that made me first your slave,
I should in thought controule your times of pleasure,
Or at your hand th'account of houres to crave,
Being your vassail bound to staie your leisure.
Oh let me suffer (being at your beck)
Th'imprison'd absence of your libertie,
And patience tame, to sufferance bide each check,
Without accusing you of injury.
Be where you list, your charter is so strong,
That you your selfe may priviledge your time
To what you will, to you it doth belong,
Your selfe to pardon of selfe-doing crime.
    I am to waite, though waiting so be hell,
    Not blame your pleasure be it ill or well.

If their bee nothing new, but that which is,
Hath beene before, how are our braines beguild,
Which laboring for invention beare amisse
The second burthen of a former child?
Oh that record could with a back-ward looke,
Even of five hundreth courses of the Sunne,
Show me your image in some antique booke,
Since minde at first in carrecter was done.
That I might see what the old world could say,
To this composed wonder of your frame,
Whether we are mended, or where better they,
Or whether revolution be the same.
    Oh sure I am the wits of former daies,
    To subjects worse have given admiring praise.

Like as the waves make towards the pibled shore,
So do our minuites hasten to their end,
Each changing place with that which goes before,
In sequent toile all forwards do contend.
Nativity once in the maine of light.
Crawles to maturity, wherewith being crown'd,
Crooked eclipses gainst his glory fight,
And time that gave, doth now his gift confound.
Time doth transfixe the florish set on youth,
And delves the paralels in beauties brow,
Feedes on the rarities of natures truth,
And nothing stands but for his sieth to mow.
  And yet to times in hope, my verse shall stand
  Praising thy worth, dispight his cruell hand.

Is it thy wil, thy Image should keepe open
My heavy eielids to the weary night?
Dost thou desire my slumbers should be broken,
While shadowes like to thee do mocke my sight?
Is it thy spirit that thou send'st from thee
So farre from home into my deeds to prye,
To find out shames and idle houres in me,
The skope and tenure of thy Jelousie?
O no, thy love though much, is not so great,
It is my love that keepes mine eie awake,
Mine owne true love that doth my rest defeat,
To plaie the watch-man ever for thy sake.
  For thee watch I, whilst thou dost wake elsewhere,
  From me farre of, with others all to neere.

Sinne of self-love possesseth al mine eie,
And all my soule, and al my every part;
And for this sinne there is no remedie,
It is so grounded inward in my heart.
Me thinkes no face so gratious is as mine,
No shape so true, no truth of such account,
And for my selfe mine owne worth do define,
As I all other in all worths surmount.
But when my glasse shewes me my selfe indeed
Beated and chopt with tand antiquitie,
Mine owne selfe love quite contrary I read
Selfe, so selfe loving were iniquity,
  T'is thee (my selfe) that for my selfe I praise,
  Painting my age with beauty of thy daies,

Against my love shall be as I am now
With times injurious hand chrusht and ore-worne,
When houres have dreind his blood and fild his brow
With lines and wrincles, when his youthfull morne
Hath travaild on to Ages steepie night,
And all those beauties whereof now he's King
Are vanishing, or vanisht out of sight,
Stealing away the treasure of his Spring.
For such a time do I now fortifie
Against confounding Ages cruell knife,
That he shall never cut from memory
My sweet loves beauty, though my lovers life.
    His beautie shall in these blacke lines be seene,
    And they shall live, and he in them still greene.

When I have seene by times fell hand defaced
The rich proud cost of outworne buried age,
When sometime loftie towers I see downe rased,
And brasse eternall slave to mortall rage.
When I have seene the hungry Ocean gaine
Advantage on the Kingdome of the shoare,
And the firme soile win of the watry maine,
Increasing store with losse, and losse with store.
When I have seene such interchange of state,
Or state it selfe confounded, to decay,
Ruine hath taught me thus to ruminate
That Time will come and take my love away.
  This thought is as a death which cannot choose
  But weepe to have, that which it feares to loose.

Since brasse, nor stone, nor earth, nor boundlesse sea,
But sad mortallity ore-swaies their power,
How with this rage shall beautie hold a plea,
Whose action is no stronger then a flower?
O how shall summers hunny breath hold out,
Against the wrackfull siedge of battring dayes,
When rocks impregnable are not so stoute,
Nor gates of steele so strong but time decayes?
O fearefull meditation, where alack,
Shall times best Jewell from times chest lie hid?
Or what strong hand can hold his swift foote back,
Or who his spoile or beautie can forbid?
    O none, unlesse this miracle have might,
    That in black inck my love may still shine bright.

Tyr'd with all these for restfull death I cry,
As to behold desert a begger borne,
And needie Nothing trimd in jollitie,
And purest faith unhappily forsworne,
And gilded honor shamefully misplast,
And maiden vertue rudely strumpeted,
And right perfection wrongfully disgrac'd,
And strength by limping sway disabled,
And arte made tung-tide by authoritie,
And Folly (Doctor-like) controuling skill,
And simple-Truth miscalde Simplicitie,
And captive-good attending Captaine ill.
  Tyr'd with all these, from these would I be gone,
  Save that to dye, I leave my love alone.

Ah wherefore with infection should he live,
And with his presence grace impietie,
That sinne by him advantage should atchive,
And lace it selfe with his societie?
Why should false painting immitate his cheeke,
And steale dead seeing of his living hew?
Why should poore beautie indirectly seeke,
Roses of shaddow, since his Rose is true?
Why should he live, now nature banckrout is,
Beggerd of blood to blush through lively vaines,
For she hath no exchecker now but his,
And proud of many, lives upon his gaines?
    O him she stores, to show what welth she had,
    In daies long since, before these last so bad.

Thus is his cheeke the map of daies out-worne,
When beauty liv'd and dy'ed as flowers do now,
Before these bastard signes of faire were borne,
Or durst inhabit on a living brow:
Before the goulden tresses of the dead,
The right of sepulchers, were shorne away,
To live a scond life on second head,
Ere beauties dead fleece made another gay:
In him those holy antique howers are seene,
Without all ornament, it selfe and true,
Making no summer of an others greene,
Robbing no ould to dresse his beauty new,
    And him as for a map doth Nature store,
    To shew faulse Art what beauty was of yore.

Those parts of thee that the worlds eye doth view,
Want nothing that the thought of hearts can mend:
All toungs (the voice of soules) give thee that end,
Uttring bare truth, even so as foes Commend.
Their outward thus with outward praise is crownd,
But those same toungs that give thee so thine owne,
In other accents doe this praise confound
By seeing farther then the eye hath showne.
They looke into the beauty of thy mind,
And that in guesse they measure by thy deeds,
Then churls their thoughts (although their eies were kind)
To thy faire flower ad the rancke smell of weeds,
      But why thy odor matcheth not thy show,
      The solye is this, that thou doest common grow.

That thou are blam'd shall not be thy defect,
For slanders marke was ever yet the faire,
The ornament of beauty is suspect,
A Crow that flies in heavens sweetest ayre.
So thou be good, slander doth but approve,
Their worth the greater beeing woo'd of time,
For Canker vice the sweetest buds doth love,
And thou present'st a pure unstayined prime.
Thou hast past by the ambush of young daies,
Either not assayld, or victor beeing charg'd,
Yet this thy praise cannot be soe thy praise,
To tye up envy, evermore inlarged,
    If some suspect of ill maskt not thy show,
    Then thou alone kingdomes of hearts shouldst owe.

Noe Longer mourne for me when I am dead,
Then you shall heare the surly sullen bell
Give warning to the world that I am fled
From this vile world with vildest wormes to dwell:
Nay if you read this line, remember not,
The hand that writ it, for I love you so,
That I in your sweet thoughts would be forgot,
If thinking on me then should make you woe.
O if (I say) you looke upon this verse,
When I (perhaps) compounded am with clay,
Do not so much as my poore name reherse;
But let your love even with my life decay.
  Least the wise world should looke into your mone,
  And mocke you with me after I am gon.

O least the world should taske you to recite,
What merit liv'd in me that you should love
After my death (deare love) for get me quite,
For you in me can nothing worthy prove.
Unlesse you would devise some vertuous lye,
To doe more for me then mine owne desert,
And hang more praise upon deceased I,
Then nigard truth would willingly impart:
O least your true love may seeme falce in this,
That you for love speake well of me untrue,
My name be buried where my body is,
And live no more to shame nor me, nor you.
  For I am shamd by that which I bring forth,
  And so should you, to love things nothing worth.

73

That time of yeeare thou maist in me behold,
When yellow leaves, or none, or few doe hange
Upon those boughes which shake against the could,
Bare rn'wd quiers, where late the sweet birds sang.
In me thou seest the twi-light of such day,
As after Sun-set fadeth in the West,
Which by and by blacke night doth take away,
Deaths second selfe that seals up all in rest.
In me thou seest the glowing of such fire,
That on the ashes of his youth doth lye,
As the death bed, whereon it must expire,
Consum'd with that which it was nurrisht by.
  This thou percev'st, which makes thy love more strong,
  To love that well, which thou must leave ere long.

But be contented when that fell arest,
With out all bayle shall carry me away,
My life hath in this line some interest,
Which for memoriall still with thee shall stay.
When thou revewest this, thou doest revew,
The very part was consecrate to thee,
The earth can have but earth, which is his due,
My spirit is thine the better part of me,
So then thou hast but lost the dregs of life,
The pray of wormes, my body being dead,
The coward conquest of a wretches knife,
To base of thee to be remembred,
  The worth of that, is that which it containes,
  And that is this, and this with thee remaines.

So are you to my thoughts as food to life,
Or as sweet season'd shewers are to the ground;
And for the peace of you I hold such strife,
As twixt a miser and his wealth is found.
Now proud as an injoyer, and anon
Doubting the filching age will steale his treasure,
Now counting best to be with you alone,
Then betterd that the world may see my pleasure,
Some-time all ful with feasting on your sight,
And by and by cleane starved for a looke,
Possessing or pursuing no delight
Save what is had, or must from you be tooke.
    Thus do I pine and surfet day by day,
      Or gluttoning on all, or all away,

Why is my verse so barren of new pride?
So far from variation or quicke change?
Why with the time do I not glance aside
To new found methods, and to compounds strange?
Why write I still all one, ever the same,
And keepe invention in a noted weed,
That every word doth almost fel my name,
Shewing their birth, and where they did proceed?
O know sweet love I alwaies write of you,
And you and love are still my argument:
So all my best is dressing old words new,
Spending againe what is already spent:
    For as the Sun is daily new and old,
    So is my love still telling what is told,

Thy glasse will shew thee how thy beauties were,
Thy dyall how thy pretious mynuits waste,
The vacant leaves thy mindes imprint will beare,
And of this booke, this learning maist thou taste.
The wrinckles which thy glasse will truly show,
Of mouthed graves will give thee memorie,
Thou by thy dyals shady stealth maist know,
Times theevish progresse to eternitie.
Looke what thy memorie cannot containe,
Commit to these waste blacks, and thou shalt finde
Those children nurst, deliverd from thy braine,
To take a new acquaintance of thy minde.
    These offices, so oft as thou wilt looke,
    Shall profit thee, and much inrich thy booke.

So oft have I invok'd thee for my Muse,
And found such faire assistance in my verse,
As every *Alien* pen hath got my use,
And under thee their poesie disperse.
Thine eyes, that taught the dumbe on high to sing,
And heavie ignorance aloft to flie,
Have added fethers to the learneds wing,
And given grace a double Majestie.
Yet be most proud of that which I compile,
Whose influence is thine, and borne of thee,
In others workes thou doost but mend the stile,
And Arts with thy sweete graces graced be.
    But thou art all my art, and doost advance
    As high as learning, my rude ignorance.

Whilst I alone did call upon thy ayde,
My verse alone had all thy gentle grace,
But now my gracious numbers are decayde,
And my sick Muse doth give an other place.
I grant (sweet love) thy lovely argument
Deserves the travaile of a worthier pen,
Yet what of thee thy Poet doth invent,
He robs thee of, and payes it thee againe,
He lends thee vertue, and he stole that word,
From thy behaviour, beautie doth he give
And found it in thy cheeke: he can affoord
No praise to thee, but what in thee doth live.
  Then thanke him not for that which he doth say,
  Since what he owes thee, thou thy selfe doost pay,

O how I faint when I of you do write,
Knowing a better spirit doth use your name,
And in the praise thereof spends all his might,
To make me toung-tide speaking of your fame.
But since your worth (wide as the Ocean is)
The humble as the proudest saile doth beare,
My sawsie barke (inferior farre to his)
On your broad maine doth wilfully appeare.
Your shallowest helpe will hold me up a floate,
Whilst he upon your soundlesse deepe doth ride,
Or (being wrackt) I am a worthlesse bote,
He of tall building, and of goodly pride.
    Then If he thrive and I be cast away,
    The worst was this, my love was my decay.

Or I shall live your Epitaph to make,
Or you survive when I in earth am rotten,
From hence your memory death cannot take,
Although in me each part will be forgotten.
Your name from hence immortall life shall have,
Though I (once gone) to all the world must dye,
The earth can yeeld me but a common grave,
When you intombed in mens eyes shall lye,
Your monument shall be my gentle verse,
Which eyes not yet created shall ore-read,
And toungs to be, your beeing shall rehearse,
When all the breathers of this world are dead,
    You still shall live (such vertue hath my Pen)
    Where breath most breaths, even in the mouths of men.

I grant thou wert not married to my Muse,
And therefore maiest without attaint ore-looke
The dedicated words which writers use
Of their faire subject, blessing every booke.
Thou art as faire in knowledge as in hew,
Finding thy worth a limmit past my praise,
And therefore art inforc'd to seeke anew,
Some fresher stampe of the time bettering dayes.
And do so love, yet when they have devisde,
What strained touches Rhethorick can lend,
Thou truly faire, wert truly simpathizde,
In true plaine words, by thy true telling friend.
   And their grosse painting might be better us'd,
   Where cheekes need blood, in thee it is abus'd.

I never saw that you did painting need,
And therefore to your faire no painting set,
I found (or thought I found) you did exceed,
The barren tender of a Poets debt:
And therefore have I slept in your report,
That you your selfe being extant well might show,
How farre a moderne quill doth come to short,
Speaking of worth, what worth in you doth grow,
This silence for my sinne you did impute,
Which shall be most my glory being dombe,
For I impaire not beautie being mute,
When others would give life, and bring a tombe.
    There lives more life in one of your faire eyes,
    Then both your Poets can in praise devise.

Who is it that sayes most, which can say more,
Then this rich praise, that you alone, are you,
In whose confine immured is the store,
Which should example where your equall grew,
Leane penurie within that Pen doth dwell,
That to his subject lends not some small glory,
But he that writes of you, if he can tell,
That you are you, so dignifies his story.
Let him but coppy what in you is writ,
Not making worse what nature made so cleere,
And such a counter-part shall fame his wit,
Making his stile admired every where.
    You to your beautious blessings adde a curse,
    Being fond on praise, which makes your praises worse.

My toung-tide Muse in manners holds her still,
While comments of your praise richly compil'd,
Reserve their Character with goulden quill,
And precious phrase by all the Muses fil'd.
I thinke good thoughts, whilst other write good wordes,
And like unlettered clarke still crie Amen,
To every Himne that able spirit affords,
In polisht forme of well refined pen.
Hearing you praisd, I say 'tis so, 'tis true,
And to the most of praise adde some-thing more,
But that is in my thought, whose love to you
(Though words come hind-most) holds his ranke before,
    Then others, for the breath of words respect,
    Me for my dombe thoughts, speaking in effect.

Was it the proud full saile of his great verse,
Bound for the prize of (all to precious) you,
That did my ripe thoughts in my braine inhearce,
Making their tombe the wombe wherein they grew?
Was it his spirit, by spirits taught to write,
Above a mortall pitch, that struck me dead?
No, neither he, nor his compiers by night
Giving him ayde, my verse astonished.
He nor that affable familiar ghost
Which nightly gulls him with intelligence,
As victors of my silence cannot boast,
I was not sick of any feare from thence.
    But when your countinance fild up his line,
    Then lackt I matter, that infeebled mine.

87

Farewell thou art too deare for my possessing,
And like enough thou knowst thy estimate,
The Charter of thy worth gives thee releasing:
My bonds in thee are all determinate.
For how do I hold thee but by thy granting,
And for that ritches where is my deserving?
The cause of this faire guift in me is wanting,
And so my pattent back againe is swerving.
Thy selfe thou gav'st, thy owne worth then not knowing,
Or mee to whom thou gav'st it, else mistaking,
So thy great guift upon misprision growing,
Comes home againe, on better judgement making.
    Thus have I had thee as a dreame doth flatter,
    In sleepe a King, but waking no such matter.

When thou shalt be dispode to set me light,
And place my merrit in the eie of skorne,
Upon thy side, against my selfe ile fight,
And prove thee virtuous, though thou art forsworne:
With mine owne weakenesse being best acquainted,
Upon thy part I can set downe a story
Of faults conceald, wherein I am attainted:
That thou in loosing me, shall win much glory:
And I by this wil be a gainer too,
For bending all my loving thoughts on thee,
The injuries that to my selfe I doe,
Doing thee vantage, duble vantage me.
    Such is my love, to thee I so belong,
    That for thy right, my selfe will beare all wrong.

Say that thou didst forsake mee for some falt,
And I will comment upon that offence,
Speake of my lamenesse, and I straight will halt:
Against thy reasons making no defence.
Thou canst not (love) disgrace me halfe so ill,
To set a forme upon desired change,
As ile my selfe disgrace, knowing thy wil,
I will acquaintance strangle and looke strange:
Be absent from thy walkes and in my tongue,
Thy sweet beloved name no more shall dwell,
Least I (too much prophane) should do it wronge:
And haplie of our old acquaintance tell.
    For thee, against my selfe ile vow debate,
    For I must nere love him whom thou dost hate.

Then hate me when thou wilt, if ever, now,
Now while the world is bent my deeds to crosse,
Joyne with the spight of fortune, make me bow,
And doe not drop in for an after losse:
Ah doe not, when my heart hath scapte this sorrow,
Come in the rereward of a conquerd woe,
Give not a windy night a rainie morrow,
To linger out a purposd over-throw.
If thou wilt leave me, do not leave me last,
When other pettie griefes have done their spight,
But in the onset come, so stall I taste
At first the very worst of fortunes might.
　　And other straines of woe, which now seeme woe,
　　Compar'd with losse of thee, will not seeme so.

91

Some glory in their birth, some in their skill,
Some in their wealth, some in their bodies force,
Some in their garments though new-fangled ill:
Some in their Hawkes and Hounds, some in their Horse.
And every humor hath his adjunct pleasure,
Wherein it findes a joy above the rest,
But these perticulers are not my measure,
All these I better in one generall best.
Thy love is bitter then high birth to me,
Richer then wealth, prouder then garments cost,
Of more delight then Hawkes or Horses bee:
And having thee, of all mens pride I boast.
    Wretched in this alone, that thou maist take,
    All this away, and me most wretched make.

But doe thy worst to steale thy selfe away,
For tearme of life thou art assured mine,
And life no longer then thy love will stay,
For it depends upon that love of thine.
Then need I not to feare the worst of wrongs,
When in the least of them my life hath end,
I see, a better state to me belongs
Then that, which on thy humor doth depend.
Thou canst not vex me with inconstant minde,
Since that my life on thy revolt doth lie,
Oh what a happy title do I finde,
Happy to have thy love, happy to die!
  But whats so blessed faire that feares no blot,
  Thou maist be falce, and yet I know it not.

So shall I live, supposing thou art true,
Like a deceived husband, so loves face,
May still seeme love to me, though alter'd new:
Thy lookes with me, thy heart in other place.
For their can live no hatred in thine eye,
Therefore in that I cannot know thy change,
In manies lookes, the falce hearts history
Is writ in moods and frounes and wrinckles strange.
But heaven in thy creation did decree,
That in thy face sweet love should ever dwell,
What ere thy thoughts, or thy hearts workings be,
Thy lookes should nothing thence, but sweetnesse tell.
    How like *Eaves* apple doth thy beauty grow,
    If thy sweet vertue answere not thy show.

They that have powre to hurt, and will doe none,
That doe not do the thing, they most do showe,
Who moving others, are themselves as stone,
Unmooved, could, and to temptation slow:
They rightly do inherrit heavens graces,
And husband natures ritches from expence,
They are the Lords and owners of their faces,
Others, but stewards of their excellence:
The sommers flowre is to the sommer sweet,
Though to it selfe, it onely live and die,
But if that flowre with base infection meete,
The basest weed out-braves his dignity:
    For sweetest things turne sowrest by their deedes,
    Lillies that fester, smell far worse then weeds.

How sweet and lovely dost thou make the shame,
Which like a canker in the fragrant Rose,
Doth spot the beautie of thy budding name?
Oh in what sweets doest thou thy sinnes inclose!
That tongue that tells the story of thy daies,
(Making lascivious comments on thy sport)
Cannot dispraise, but in a kinde of praise,
Naming thy name, blesses an ill report.
Oh what a mansion have those vices got,
Which for their habitation chose out thee,
Where beauties vaile doth cover every blot,
And all things turnes to faire, that eies can see!
    Take heed (deare heart) of this large priviledge,
    The hardest knife ill us'd doth loose his edge.

96

Some say thy fault is youth, some wantonesse,
Some say thy grace is youth and gentle sport,
Both grace and faults are lov'd of more and lesse:
Thou makst faults graces, that to thee resort:
As on the finger of a throned Queene,
The basest Jewell wil be well esteem'd:
So are those errors that in thee are seene,
To truths translated, and for true things deem'd.
How many Lambs might the sterne Wolfe betray,
If like a Lambe he could his lookes translate.
How many gazers mighst thou lead away,
If thou wouldst use the strength of all thy state?
     But doe not so, I love thee in such sort,
     As thou being mine, mine is thy good report.

97

How like a Winter hath my absence beene
From thee, the pleasure of the fleeting yeare?
What freezings have I felt, what darke daies seene?
What old Decembers barenesse every where?
And yet this time remov'd was sommers time,
The teeming Autumne big with ritch increase,
Bearing the wanton burthen of the prime,
Like widdowed wombes after their Lords decease:
Yet this aboundant issue seem'd to me,
But hope of Orphans, and un-fathered fruite,
For Sommer and his pleasures waite on thee,
And thou away, the very birds are mute.
  Or if they sing, tis with so dull a cheere,
  That leaves looke pale, dreading the Winters neere.

98

From you have I beene absent in the spring,
When proud pide Aprill (drest in all his trim)
Hath put a spirit of youth in every thing:
That heavie *Saturne* laught and leapt with him.
Yet nor the laies of birds, nor the sweet smell
Of different flowers in odor and in hew, ·
Could make me any summers story tell:
Or from their proud lap pluck them where they grew:
Nor did I wonder at the Lillies white,
Nor praise the deepe vermillion in the Rose,
They weare but sweet, but figures of delight:
Drawne after you, you patterne of all those.
    Yet seem'd it Winter still, and you away,
    As with your shaddow I with these did play.

99

The forward violet thus did I chide,
Sweet theefe whence didst thou steale thy sweet that
If not from my loves breath, the purple pride, (smels
Which on thy soft cheeke for complexion dwells?
In my loves veines thou hast too grosely died,
The Lillie I condemned for thy hand,
And buds of marjerom had stolne thy haire,
The Roses fearefully on thornes did stand,
Our blushing shame, an other white dispaire:
A third nor red, nor white, had stolne of both,
And to his robbry had annext thy breath,
But for his theft in pride of all his growth
A vengfull canker eate him up to death.
    More flowers I noted, yet I none could see,
    But sweet, or culler it had stolne from thee.

Where art thou Muse that thou forgetst so long,
To speake of that which gives thee all thy might?
Spendst thou thy furie on some worthlesse songe,
Darkning thy powre to lend base subjects light.
Returne forgetfull Muse, and straight redeeme,
In gentle numbers time so idely spent,
Sing to the eare that doth thy laies esteeme,
And gives thy pen both skill and argument.
Rise resty Muse, my loves sweet face survay,
If time have any wrincle graven there,
If any, be a *Satire* to decay,
And make times spoiles dispised every where.
    Give my love fame faster then time wasts life,
    So thou prevenst his sieth, and crooked knife.

101

Oh truant Muse what shalbe thy amends,
For thy neglect of truth in beauty di'd?
Both truth and beauty on my love depends:
So dost thou too, and therein dignifi'd:
Make answere Muse, wilt thou not haply saie,
Truth needs no collour with his collour fixt,
Beautie no pensell, beauties truth to lay:
But best is best, if never intermixt.
Because he needs no praise, wilt thou be dumb?
Excuse not silence so, for't lies in thee,
To make him much out-live a gilded tombe:
And to be praisd of ages yet to be.
  Then do thy office Muse, I teach thee how,
  To make him seeme long hence, as he showes now.

102

My love is strengthned though more weake in see-
I love not lesse, thogh lesse the show appeare, (ming
That love is marchandiz'd, whose ritch esteeming,
The owners tongue doth publish every where.
Our love was new, and then but in the spring,
When I was wont to greet it with my laies,
As *Philomell* in summers front doth singe,
And stops his pipe in growth of riper daies:
Not that the summer is lesse pleasant now
Then when her mournefull himns did hush the night,
But that wild musick burthens every bow,
And sweets growne common loose their deare delight.
　　Therefore like her, I some-time hold my tongue:
　　Because I would not dull you with my songe.

Alack what poverty my Muse brings forth,
That having such a skope to show her pride,
The argument all bare is of more worth
Then when it hath my added praise beside.
Oh blame me not if I no more can write!
Looke in your glasse and there appeares a face,
That over-goes my blunt invention quite,
Dulling my lines, and doing me disgrace.
Were it not sinfull then striving to mend,
To marre the subject that before was well,
For to no other passe my verses tend,
Then of your graces and your gifts to tell.
    And more, much more then in my verse can sit,
    Your owne glasse showes you, when you looke in it.

104

To me faire friend you never can be old,
For as you were when first your eye I eyde,
Such seemes your beautie still: Three Winters colde,
Have from the forrests shooke three summers pride,
Three beautious springs to yellow *Autumne* turned,
In processe of the seasons have I seene,
Three Aprill perfumes in three hot Junes burn'd,
Since first I saw you fresh which yet are greene.
Ah yet doth beauty like a Dyall hand,
Steale from his figure, and no pace perceiv'd,
So your sweete hew, which me thinkes still doth stand
Hath motion, and mine eye may be deceaved.
    For feare of which, heare this thou age unbred,
    Ere you were borne was beauties summer dead.

Let not my love be cal'd Idolatrie,
Nor my beloved as an Idoll show,
Since all alike my songs and praises be
To one, of one, still such, and ever so.
Kinde is my love to day, to morrow kinde,
Still constant in a wondrous excellence.
Therefore my verse to constancie confin'de,
One thing expressing, leaves out difference.
Faire, kinde, and true, is all my argument,
Faire, kinde and true, varrying to other words,
And in this change is my invention spent,
Three theams in one, which wondrous scope affords.
    Faire, kinde, and true, have often liv'd alone.
    Which three till now, never kept seate in one.

106

When in the Chronicle of wasted time,
 I see discriptions of the fairest wights,
And beautie making beautifull old rime,
 In praise of Ladies dead, and lovely Knights,
Then in the blazon of sweet beauties best,
Of hand, of foote, of lip, of eye, of brow,
 I see their antique Pen would have exprest,
Even such a beauty as you maister now.
So all their praises are but prophesies
Of this our time, all you prefiguring,
And for they look'd but with devining eyes,
They had not still enough your worth to sing:
  For we which now behold these present dayes,
  Have eyes to wonder, but lack toungs to praise.

107

Not mine owne feares, nor the prophetick soule,
Of the wide world, dreaming on things to come,
Can yet the lease of my true love controule,
Supposde as forfeit to a confin'd doome.
The mortall Moone hath her eclipse indur'de,
And the sad Augurs mock their owne presage,
Incertenties now crowne them-selves assur'de,
And peace proclaimes Olives of endlesse age,
Now with the drops of this most balmie time,
My love lookes fresh, and death to me subscribes,
Since spight of him Ile live in this poore rime,
While he insults ore dull and speachlesse tribes.
  And thou in this shalt finde thy monument,
  When tyrants crests and tombs of brasse are spent.

108

What's in the braine that Inck may character,
Which hath not figur'd to thee my true spirit,
What's new to speake, what now to register,
That may expresse my love, or thy deare merit?
Nothing sweet boy, but yet like prayers divine,
I must each day say ore the very same,
Counting no old thing old, thou mine, I thine,
Even as when first I hallowed thy faire name.
So that eternall love in loves fresh case,
Waighes not the dust and injury of age,
Nor gives to necessary wrinckles place,
But makes antiquitie for aye his page,
  Finding the first conceit of love there bred,
  Where time and outward forme would shew it dead,

109

O never say that I was false of heart,
Though absence seem'd my flame to quallifie,
As easie might I from my selfe depart,
As from my soule which in thy brest doth lye:
That is my home of love, if I have rang'd,
Like him that travels I returne againe,
Just to the time, not with the time exchang'd,
So that my selfe bring water for my staine,
Never beleeve though in my nature raign'd,
All frailties that besiege all kindes of blood,
That it could so preposterouslie be stain'd,
To leave for nothing all thy summe of good:
    For nothing this wide Universe I call,
    Save thou my Rose, in it thou art my all.

Alas 'tis true, I have gone here and there,
And made my selfe a motley to the view,
Gor'd mine own thoughts, sold cheap what is most deare,
Made old offences of affections new.
Most true it is, that I have lookt on truth
Asconce and strangely: But by all above,
These blenches gave my heart an other youth,
And worse essaies prov'd thee my best of love,
Now all is done, have what shall have no end,
Mine appetite I never more will grin'de
On newer proofe, to trie an older friend,
A God in love, to whom I am confin'd.
    Then give me welcome, next my heaven the best,
    Even to thy pure and most most loving brest.

111

O for my sake doe you wish fortune chide,
The guiltie goddesse of my harmfull deeds,
That did not better for my life provide,
Then publick meanes which publick manners breeds.
Thence comes it that my name receives a brand,
And almost thence my nature is subdu'd
To what it workes in, like the Dyers hand,
Pitty me then, and wish I were renu'de,
Whilst like a willing pacient I will drinke,
Potions of Eysell gainst my strong infection,
No bitternesse that I will bitter thinke,
Nor double pennance to correct correction.
    Pittie me then deare friend, and I assure yee,
    Even that your pittie is enough to cure mee.

Your love and pittie doth th'impression fill,
Which vulgar scandall stampt upon my brow,
For what care I who calles me well or ill,
So you ore-greene my bad, my good alow?
You are my All the world, and I must strive,
To know my shames and praises from your tounge,
None else to me, nor I to none alive,
That my steel'd sence or changes right or wrong,
In so profound *Abisme* I throw all care
Of others voyces, that my Adders sence,
To cryttick and to flatterer stopped are:
Marke how with my neglect I doe dispence.
    You are so strongly in my purpose bred,
    That all the world besides me thinkes y'are dead.

113

Since I left you, mine eye is in my minde,
And that which governes me to goe about,
Doth part his function, and is partly blind,
Seemes seeing, but effectually is out:
For it no forme delivers to the heart
Of bird, of flowre, or shape which it doth lack,
Of his quick objects hath the minde no part,
Nor his owne vision houlds what it doth catch:
For if it see the rud'st or gentlest sight,
The most sweet-favor or deformedst creature,
The mountaine, or the sea, the day, or night:
The Croe, or Dove, it shapes them to your feature.
   Incapable of more repleat, with you,
   My most true minde thus maketh mine untrue.

114

Or whether doth my minde being crown'd with you
Drinke up the monarks plague this flattery?
Or whether shall I say mine eie saith true,
And that your love taught it this *Alcumie?*
To make of monsters, and things indigest,
Such cherubines as your sweet selfe resemble,
Creating every bad a perfect best
As fast as objects to his beames assemble:
Oh tis the first, tis flatry in my seeing,
And my great minde most kingly drinkes it up,
Mine eie well knowes what with his gust is greeing,
And to his pallat doth prepare the cup.
  If it be poison'd, tis the lesser sinne,
    That mine eye loves it and doth first beginne.

Those lines that I before have writ doe lie,
Even those that said I could not love you deerer,
Yet then my judgement knew no reason why,
My most full flame should afterwards burne cleerer.
But reckening time, whose milliond accidents
Creepe in twixt vowes, and change decrees of Kings,
Tan sacred beautie, blunt the sharp'st intents,
Divert strong mindes to th'course of altring things:
Alas why fearing of times tiranie,
Might I not then say now I love you best,
When I was certaine ore in-certainty,
Crowning the present, doubting of the rest:
    Love is a Babe, then might I not say so
    To give full growth to that which still doth grow.

Let me not to the marriage of true mindes
Admit impediments, love is not love
Which alters when it alteration findes,
Or bends with the remover to remove.
O no, it is an ever fixed marke
 That lookes on tempests and is never shaken;
It is the star to every wandring barke,
Whose worths unknowne, although his higth be taken.
Lov's not Times foole, though rosie lips and cheeks
Within his bending sickles compasse come,
Love alters not with his breefe houres and weekes,
But beares it out even to the edge of doome:
        If this be error and upon me proved,
        I never writ, nor no man ever loved.

117

Accuse me thus, that I have scanted all,
Wherein I should your great deserts repay,
Forgot upon your dearest love to call,
Whereto al bonds do tie me day by day,
That I have frequent binne with unknown mindes,
And given to time your owne deare purchas'd right,
That I have hoysted saile to al the windes
Which should transport me farthest from your sight.
Booke both my wilfulnesse and errors downe,
And on just proofe surmise, accumilate,
Bring me within the level of your frowne,
But shoote not at me in your wakened hate:
    Since my appeale saies I did strive to proove
    The constancy and virtue of your love

118

Like as to make our appetites more keene
With eager compounds we our pallat urge,
As to prevent our malladies unseene,
We sicken to shun sicknesse when we purge.
Even so being full of your nere cloying sweetnesse,
To bitter sawces did I frame my feeding;
And sicke of wel-fare found a kind of meetnesse,
To be diseas'd ere that there was true needing.
Thus pollicie in love t'anticipate
The ills that were, not grew to faults assured,
And brought to medicine a healthfull state
Which rancke of goodnesse would by ill be cured.
  But thence I learne and find the lesson true,
  Drugs poyson him that so fell sicke of you.

119

What potions have I drunke of *Syren* teares
Distil'd from Lymbecks foule as hell within,
Applying feares to hopes, and hopes to feares,
Still loosing when I saw my selfe to win?
What wretched errors hath my heart committed,
Whilst it hath thought it selfe so blessed never?
How have mine eies out of their Spheares bene fitted
In the distraction of this madding fever?
O benefit of ill, now I find true
That better is, by evil still made better.
And ruin'd love when it is built anew
Growes fairer then at first, more strong, far greater.
      So I returne rebukt to my content,
      And gaine by ills thrise more then I have spent.

That you were once unkind be-friends mee now,
And for that sorrow, which I then didde feele,
Needes must I under my transgression bow,
Unlesse my Nerves were brasse or hammered steele.
For if you were by my unkindnesse shaken
As I by yours, y'have past a hell of Time,
And I a tyrant have no leasure taken
To waigh how once I suffered in your crime.
O that our night of wo might have remembred
My deepest sence, how hard true sorrow hits,
And soone to you, as you to me then tendred
The humble salve, which wounded bosomes fits!
　　But that your trespasse now becomes a fee,
　　Mine ransoms yours, and yours must ransome mee.

'Tis better to be vile then vile esteemed,
When not to be, receives reproach of being,
And the just pleasure lost, which is so deemed,
Not by our feeling, but by others seeing.
For why should others false adulterat eyes
Give salutation to my sportive blood?
Or on my frailties why are frailer spies;
Which in their wils count bad what I think good?
Noe, I am that I am, and they that levell
At my abuses, reckon up their owne,
I may be straight though they them-selves be bevel
By their rancke thoughtes, my deedes must not be showne
    Unlesse this generall evill they maintaine,
    All men are bad and in their badnesse raigne.

TThy guift„ thy tables, are within my braine
Full characterd with lasting memory,
Which shall above that idle rancke remaine
Beyond all date, even to eternity.
Or at the least, so long as braine and heart
Have facultie by nature to subsist,
Til each to raz'd oblivion yeeld his part
Of thee, thy record never can be mist:
That poore retention could not so much hold,
Nor need I tallies thy deare love to skore,
Therefore to give them from me was I bold,
To trust those tables that receave thee more,
  To keepe an adjunckt to remember thee,
  Were to import forgetfulnesse in mee.

No! Time, thou shalt not bost that I doe change,
Thy pyramyds buylt up with newer might
To me are nothing novell, nothing strange,
They are but dressings of a former sight:
Our dates are breefe, and therefor we admire,
What thou dost foyst upon us that is ould,
And rather make them borne to our desire,
Then thinke that we before have heard them tould:
Thy registers and thee I both defie,
Not wondring at the present, nor the past,
For thy records, and what we see doth lye,
Made more or les by thy continuall hast:
    This I doe vow and this shall ever be,
    I will be true dispight thy syeth and thee.

Yf my deare love were but the childe of state,
It might for fortunes basterd be unfathered,
As subject to times love, or to times hate,
Weeds among weeds, or flowers with flowers gatherd.
No it was buylded far from accident,
It suffers not in smilinge pomp, nor falls
Under the blow of thralled discontent,
Whereto th'inviting time our fashion calls:
It feares not policy that *Heriticke*,
Which workes on leases of short numbred howers,
But all alone stands hugely pollitick,
That it nor growes with heat, nor drownes with showres.
  To this I witnes call the foles of time,
    Which die for goodnes, who have liv'd for crime.

Wer't ought to me I bore the canopy,
With my extern the outward honoring,
Or layd great bases for eternity,
Which proves more short then wast or ruining?
Have I not seene dwellers on forme and favor
Lose all, and more by paying too much rent
For compound sweet; Forgoing simple savor,
Pittifull thrivors in their gazing spent.
Noe, let me be obsequious in thy heart,
And take thou my oblacion, poore but free,
Which is not mixt with seconds, knows no art,
But mutuall render, onely me for thee.
    Hence, thou subbornd *Informer*, a trew soule
    When most impeacht, stands least in thy controule.

126

O thou my lovely Boy who in thy power,
Doest hould times fickle glasse, his sickle, hower:
Who hast by wayning growne, and therein shou'st,
Thy lovers withering, as thy sweet selfe grow'st.
If Nature (soveraine misteres over wrack)
As thou goest onwards still will plucke thee backe,
She keepes thee to this purpose, that her skill.
May time disgrace, and wretched mynuit kill.
Yet feare her O thou minnion of her pleasure,
She may detaine, but not still keepe her tresure!
   Her *Audite* (though delayd) answer'd must be,
   And her *Quietus* is to render thee.

127

In the ould age blacke was not counted faire,
Or if it weare it bore not beauties name:
But now is blacke beauties successive heire,
And Beautie slanderd with a bastard shame,
For since each hand hath put on Natures power,
Fairing the foule with Arts faulse borrow'd face,
Sweet beauty hath no name no holy boure,
But is prophan'd, if not lives in disgrace.
Therefore my Mistersse eyes are Raven blacke,
Her eyes so suted, and they mourners seeme,
At such who not borne faire no beauty lack,
Slandring Creation with a false esteeme,
  Yet so they mourne becomming of their woe,
  That every toung saies beauty should looke so.

128

How oft when thou my musike musike playst,
Upon that blessed wood whose motion sounds
With thy sweet fingers when thou gently swayst,
The wiry concord that mine eare confounds,
Do I envie those Jackes that nimble leape,
To kisse the tender inward of thy hand,
Whilst my poore lips which should that harvest reape,
At the woods bouldnes by thee blushing stand.
To be so tikled they would change their state,
And situation with those dancing chips,
Ore whome their fingers walke with gentle gate,
Making dead wood more blest then living lips,
    Since sausie Jackes so happy are in this,
    Give them their fingers, me thy lips to kisse.

129

Th'expence of Spirit in a waste of shame
Is lust in action, and till action, lust
Is perjurd, murdrous, blouddy full of blame,
Savage, extreame, rude, cruell, not to trust,
Injoyd no sooner but dispised straight,
Past reason hunted, and no sooner had
Past reason hated as a swollowed bayt,
On purpose layd to make the taker mad.
Made In pursut and in possession so,
Had, having, and in quest, to have extreame,
A blisse in proofe and proud and very wo,
Before a joy proposd behind a dreame,
  All this the world well knowes yet none knowes well,
  To shun the heaven that leads men to this hell.

130

My Mistres eyes are nothing like the Sunne,
Currall is farre more red, then her lips red,
If snow be white, why then her brests are dun:
If haires be wiers, black wiers grow on her head:
I have seene Roses damaskt, red and white,
But no such Roses see I in her cheekes,
And in some perfumes is there more delight,
Then in the breath that from my Mistres reekes.
I love to heare her speake, yet well I know,
That Musicke hath a farre more pleasing sound:
I graunt I never saw a goddesse goe,
My Mistres when shee walkes treads on the ground.
    And yet by heaven I thinke my love as rare,
    As any she beli'd with false compare.

131

Thou art as tiranous, so as thou art,
As those whose beauties proudly make them cruell;
For well thou know'st to my deare doting hart
Thou art the fairest and most precious Jewell.
Yet in good faith some say that thee behold,
Thy face hath not the power to make love grone;
To say they erre, I dare not be so bold,
Although I sweare it to my selfe alone.
And to be sure that is not false I sweare
A thousand grones but thinking on thy face,
One on anothers necke do witnesse beare
Thy blacke is fairest in my judgements place.
    In nothing art thou blacke save in thy deeds,
    And thence this slaunder as I thinke proceeds.

132

Thine eies I love, and they as pittying me,
Knowing thy heart torment me with disdaine,
Have put on black, and loving mourners bee,
Looking with pretty ruth upon my paine.
And truly not the morning Sun of Heaven
Better becomes the gray cheeks of th'East,
Nor that full Starre that ushers in the Eaven
Doth halfe that glory to the sober West
As those two morning eyes become thy face:
O let it then as well beseeme thy heart
To mourne for me since mourning doth thee grace,
And sute thy pitty like in every part.
    Then will I sweare beauty her selfe is blacke,
    And all they foule that thy complexion lacke.

133

Beshrew that heart that makes my heart to groane
For that deepe wound it gives my friend and me;
I'st not ynough to torture me alone,
But slave to slavery my sweet'st friend must be.
Me from my selfe thy cruell eye hath taken,
And my next selfe thou harder hast ingrossed,
Of him, my selfe, and thee I am forsaken,
A torment thrice three-fold thus to be crossed:
Prison my heart in thy steele bosomes warde,
But then my friends heart let my poore heart bale,
Who ere keepes me, let my heart be his garde,
Thou canst not then use rigor in my Jaile.
    And yet thou wilt, for I being pent in thee,
    Perforce am thine and all that is in me.

So now I have confest that he is thine,
And I my selfe am morgag'd to thy will,
My selfe Ile forfeit, so that other mine,
Thou wilt restore to be my comfort still:
But thou wilt not, nor he will not be free,
For thou art covetous, and he is kinde,
He learnd but suretie-like to write for me,
Under that bond that him as fast doth binde.
The statute of thy beauty thou wilt take,
Thou usurer that put'st forth all to use,
And sue a friend, came debter for my sake,
So him I loose through my unkinde abuse.
  Him have I lost, thou hast both him and me,
  He paies the whole, and yet am I not free.

135

Who ever hath her wish, thou hast thy *Will*,
And *Will* too boote, and *Will* in over-plus,
More then enough am I that vexe thee still,
To thy sweet will making addition thus.
Wilt thou whose will is large and spatious,
Not once vouchsafe to hide my will in thine,
Shall will in others seeme right gracious,
And in my will no faire acceptance shine:
The sea all water, yet receives raine still,
And in aboundance addeth to his store,
So thou beeing rich in *Will* adde to thy *Will*,
One will of mine to make thy large *Will* more.
    Let no unkinde, no faire beseechers kill,
    Thinke all but one, and me in that one *Will*.

136

If thy soule check thee that I come so neere,
Sweare to thy blind soule that I was thy *Will,*
And will thy soule knowes is admitted there,
Thus farre for love, my love-sute sweet fullfill.
Will, will fulfill the treasure of thy love,
I fill it full with wils, and my will one,
In things of great receit with ease we proove,
Among a number one is reckon'd none.
Then in the number let me passe untold,
Though in thy stores account I one must be,
For nothing hold me, so it please thee hold,
That nothing me, a some-thing sweet to thee.
  Make but my name thy love, and love that still,
  And then thou lovest me for my name is *Will.*

'Thou blinde foole love, what doost thou to mine eyes,
'That they behold and see not what they see:
'They know what beautie is, see where it lyes,
Yet what the best is, take the worst to be.
If eyes corrupt by over-partiall lookes,
Be anchord in the baye where all men ride,
Why of eyes falsehood hast thou forged hookes,
Whereto the judgement of my heart is tide?
Why should my heart thinke that a severall plot,
Which my heart knowes the wide worlds common place?
Or mine eyes seeing this, say this is not
'To put faire truth upon so foule a face,
    In things right true my heart and eyes have erred,
    And to this false plague are they now transferred.

When my love sweares that she is made of truth,
I do beleeve her though I know she lyes,
That she might thinke me some untuterd youth,
Unlearned in the worlds false subtilties.
Thus vainely thinking that she thinkes me young,
Although she knowes my dayes are past the best,
Simply I credit her false speaking tongue,
On both sides thus is simple truth supprest:
But wherefore sayes she not she is unjust?
And wherefore say not I that I am old?
O loves best habit is in seeming trust,
And age in love, loves not t'have yeares told.
   Therefore I lye with her, and she with me,
   And in our faults by lyes we flattered be.

139

O call not me to justifie the wrong,
That thy unkindnesse layes upon my heart,
Wound me not with thine eye but with thy toung,
Use power with power, and slay me not by Art,
Tell me thou lov'st else-where; but in my sight,
Deare heart forbeare to glance thine eye aside,
What needst thou wound with cunning when thy might
Is more then my ore-prest defence can bide?
Let me excuse thee, ah my love well knowes,
Her prettie lookes have beene mine enemies,
And therefore from my face she turnes my foes,
That they else-where might dart their injuries:
    Yet do not so, but since I am neere slaine,
    Kill me out-right with lookes, and rid my paine.

Be wise as thou art cruell, do not presse
My toung tide patience with too much disdaine:
Least sorrow lend me words and words expresse,
The manner of my pittie wanting paine.
If I might teach thee witte better it weare,
Though not to love, yet love to tell me so,
As testie sick-men when their deaths be neere,
No newes but health from their Phisitions know.
For if I should dispaire I should grow madde,
And in my madnesse might speake ill of thee,
Now this ill wresting world is growne so bad,
Madde slanderers by madde eares beleeved be.
  That I may not be so, nor thou be lyde,
  Beare thine eyes straight, though thy proud heart goe wide.

141

In faith I doe not love thee with mine eyes,
For they in thee a thousand errors note,
But 'tis my heart that loves what they dispise,
Who in dispight of view is pleasd to dote.
Nor are mine eares with thy toungs tune delighted,
Nor tender feeling to base touches prone,
Nor taste, nor smell, desire to be invited
To any sensuall feast with thee alone:
But my five wits, nor my five sences can
Diswade one foolish heart from serving thee,
Who leaves unswai'd the likenesse of a man,
Thy proud hearts slave and vassall wretch to be:
   Onely my plague thus farre I count my gaine,
   That she that makes me sinne, awards me paine.

142

Love is my sinne, and thy deare vertue hate,
Hate of my sinne, grounded on sinfull loving,
O but with mine, compare thou thine owne state,
And thou shalt finde it merrits not reprooving,
Or if it do, not from those lips of thine,
That have prophan'd their scarlet ornaments,
And seald false bonds of love as oft as mine,
Robd others beds revenues of their rents.
Be it lawfull I love thee as thou lov'st those,
Whome thine eyes wooe as mine importune thee,
Roote pittie in thy heart that when it growes,
Thy pitty may deserve to pittied bee.
    If thou doost seeke to have what thou doost hide,
    By selfe example mai'st thou be denide.

143

Loe as a carefull huswife runnes to catch,
One of her fethered creatures broake away,
Sets downe her babe and makes all swift dispatch
In pursuit of the thing she would have stay:
Whilst her neglected child holds her in chace,
Cries to catch her whose busie care is bent,
To follow that which flies before her face:
Not prizing her poore infants discontent;
So runst thou after that which flies from thee,
Whilst I thy babe chace thee a farre behind,
But if thou catch thy hope turne back to me:
And play the mothers part kisse me, be kind.
    So will I pray that thou maist have thy *Will*,
    If thou turne back and my loude crying still.

Two loves I have of comfort and dispaire,
Which like two spirits do sugiest me still,
The better angell is a man right faire:
The worser spirit a woman collour'd il.
To win me soone to hell my femall evill,
Tempteth my better angel from my sight,
And would corrupt my saint to be a divel:
Wooing his purity with her fowle pride.
And whether that my angel be turn'd finde,
Suspect I may, yet not directly tell,
But being both from me both to each friend,
I gesse one angel in an others hel.
  Yet this shal I nere know but live in doubt,
  Till my bad angel fire my good one out.

Those lips that Loves owne hand did make,
Breath'd forth the sound that said I hate,
To me that languisht for her sake:
But when she saw my wofull state,
Straight in her heart did mercie come,
Chiding that tongue that ever sweet,
Was usde in giving gentle dome:
And tought it thus a new to greete:
I hate she alterd with an end,
That follow'd it as gentle day,
Doth follow night who like a fiend
From heaven to hell is flowne away.
    I hate, from hate away she threw,
    And sav'd my life saying not you.

146

Poore soule the center of my sinfull earth,
My sinfull earth these rebbell powres that thee array,
Why dost thou pine within and suffer dearth
Painting thy outward walls so costlie gay?
Why so large cost having so short a lease,
Dost thou upon thy fading mansion spend?
Shall wormes inheritors of this excesse
Eate up thy charge? is this thy bodies end?
Then soule live thou upon thy servants losse,
And let that pine to aggravat thy store;
Buy tearmes divine in selling houres of drosse:
Within be fed, without be rich no more,
    So shalt thou feed on death, that feeds on men,
    And death once dead, ther's no more dying then.

147

My love is as a feaver longing still,
For that which longer nurseth the disease,
Feeding on that which doth preserve the ill,
'Th'uncertaine sicklie appetite to please:
My reason the Phisition to my love,
Angry that his prescriptions are not kept
Hath left me, and I desperate now approove,
Desire is death, which Phisick did except.
Past cure I am, now Reason is past care,
And frantick madde with ever-more unrest,
My thoughts and my discourse as mad mens are,
At randon from the truth vainely exprest.
  For I have sworne thee faire, and thought thee bright,
  Who art as black as hell, as darke as night.

148

O me! what eyes hath love put in my head,
Which have no correspondence with true sight,
Or if they have, where is my judgment fled,
That censures falsely what they see aright?
If that be faire whereon my false eyes dote,
What meanes the world to say it is not so?
If it be not, then love doth well denote,
Loves eye is not so true as all mens: no,
How can it? O how can loves eye be true,
That is so vext with watching and with teares?
No marvaile then though I mistake my view,
The sunne it selfe sees not, till heaven cleeres.
    O cunning love, with teares thou keepst me blinde,
    Least eyes well seeing thy foule faults should finde.

Canst thou O cruell, say I love thee not,
When I against my selfe with thee pertake:
Doe I not thinke on thee when I forgot
Am of my selfe, all tirant for thy sake?
Who hateth thee that I doe call my friend,
On whom froun'st thou that I doe faune upon,
Nay if thou lowrst on me doe I not spend
Revenge upon my selfe with present mone?
What merrit do I in my selfe respect,
That is so proude thy service to dispise,
When all my best doth worship thy defect,
Commanded by the motion of thine eyes.
  But love hate on for now I know thy minde,
  Those that can see thou lov'st, and I am blind.

Oh from what powre hast thou this powrefull might,
With insufficiency my heart to sway,
To make me give the lie to my true sight,
And swere that brightnesse doth not grace the day?
Whence hast thou this becomming of things il,
That in the very refuse of thy deeds,
There is such strength and warrantise of skill,
That in my minde thy worst all best exceeds?
Who taught thee how to make me love thee more,
The more I heare and see just cause of hate,
Oh though I love what others doe abhor,
With others thou shouldst not abhor my state.
   If thy unworthinesse raisd love in me,
   More worthy I to be belov'd of thee.

151

Love is too young to know what conscience is,
Yet who knowes not conscience is borne of love,
Then gentle cheater urge not my amisse,
Least guilty of my faults thy sweet selfe prove.
For thou betraying me, I doe betray
My nobler part to my grose bodies treason,
My soule doth tell my body that he may,
Triumph in love, flesh staies no farther reason.
But rysing at thy name doth point out thee,
As his triumphant prize, proud of this pride,
He is contented thy poore drudge to be
To stand in thy affaires, fall by thy side.
   No want of conscience hold it that I call,
   Her love, for whose deare love I rise and fall.

152

In loving thee thou know'st I am forsworne,
But thou art twice forsworne to me love swearing,
In act thy bed-vow broake and new faith torne,
In vowing new hate after new love bearing:
But why of two othes breach doe I accuse thee,
When I breake twenty: I am perjur'd most,
For all my vowes are othes but to misuse thee:
And all my honest faith in thee is lost.
For I have sworne deepe othes of thy deepe kindnesse:
Othes of thy love, thy truth, thy constancie,
And to inlighten thee gave eyes to blindnesse,
Or made them swere against the thing they see.
    For I have sworne thee faire: more perjurde eye,
    To swere against the truth so foule a lie.

153

Cupid laid by his brand and fell a sleepe,
A maide of Dyans this advantage found,
And his love-kindling fire did quickly steepe
In a could vallie-fountaine of that ground:
Which borrowd from this holie fire of love,
A datelesse lively heat still to indure,
And grew a seething bath which yet men prove,
Against strang malladies a soveraigne cure:
But at my mistres eie loves brand new fired,
The boy for triall needes would touch my brest,
I sick withall the helpe of bath desired,
And thether hied a sad distemperd guest.
  But found no cure, the bath for my helpe lies,
  Where Cupid got new fire; my mistres eye.

154

The little Love-God lying once a sleepe,
Laid by his side his heart inflaming brand,
Whilst many Nymphes that vou'd chast life to keep,
Came tripping by, but in her maiden hand,
The fayrest votary tooke up that fire,
Which many Legions of true hearts had warm'd,
And so the Generall of hot desire,
Was sleeping by a Virgin hand disarm'd.
This brand she quenched in a coole Well by,
Which from loves fire tooke heat perpetuall,
Growing a bath and healthfull remedy,
For men diseasd, but I my Mistrisse thrall,
    Came there for cure and this by that I prove,
    Loves fire heates water, water cooles not love.

FINIS.

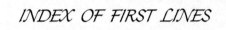

INDEX OF FIRST LINES